Dog Ado

A Guide to Choosing the Right Dog Breed for You, Welcoming Him Into Your Family and Looking After Him

By Norman Thornton

© **Copyright 2019 - All rights reserved.**

The content contained within this book may not be reproduced, duplicated or transmitted without direct written permission from the author or the publisher.

Under no circumstances will any blame or legal responsibility be held against the publisher or author for any damages, reparation, or monetary loss due to the information contained within this book. Either directly or indirectly.

Legal Notice:

This book is copyright protected. This book is only for personal use. You cannot amend, distribute, sell, use, quote or paraphrase any part, or the content within this book, without the consent of the author or publisher.

Disclaimer Notice:

Please note the information contained within this document is for educational and entertainment purposes only. All effort has been executed to present accurate, up to date and reliable, complete information. No warranties of any kind are declared or implied. Readers acknowledge that the author is not engaging in the rendering of legal, financial, medical or professional advice. The content within this book has been derived from various sources. Please consult a licensed professional before attempting any techniques outlined in this book.

By reading this document, the reader agrees that under no

circumstances is the author responsible for any losses, direct or indirect, which are incurred as a result of the use of information contained within this document, including, but not limited to, —errors, omissions, or inaccuracies.

Contents

Introduction 1

Chapter 1: Breed Comparison 4

Chapter 2: Mixed Breed Consideration 7

Chapter 3: Being Reasonable 10

Chapter 4: Networking 15

Chapter 5: Doing the Research 18

Chapter 6: Getting to Know Your Dog 23

Chapter 7: Getting Ready for the New Dog! 28

Chapter 8: Buying the Supplies 33

Chapter 9: Where to Find Breeders? 39

Chapter 10: Is Your Dog Well? 45

Chapter 11: Your Dog is an Investment! 51

Concluding Chapter: Bringing Him Home 56

Thank you for buying this book and I hope that you will find it useful. If you will want to share your thoughts on this book, you can do so by leaving a review on the Amazon page, it helps me out a lot.

Introduction

When you intend to adopt a dog, there are certain really essential points to remember to encertain that you are pleased with your brand-new dog. They could imply the distinction in between regretting your choice and having a terrific brand-new buddy whom you are going to enjoy and treasure.

One error to stay away from is purchasing a dog on the spur of the moment. You might see a dog in a pet store, or read an advertisement in the newspaper, and choose that you definitely need to own that dog. A rash decision in buying a brand-new dog is never ever a great idea. Rather, you ought to go through this guide, find out all there is to know about the dog breed you are considering, and choose if he is going suit well into your house and your life.

A second error is to underestimate the expense of a brand-new dog. Whether you select a pricey purebred or a mixed breed, purchasing a dog is far from being the only expense included. Your dog is going to require food and other products, and visits to the vet. As you desire your dog to constantly be in great condition as when you initially purchased him, you want to know that you can afford his maintenance.

Another factor in disappointment is attempting to recreate a relationship you had with a dog in your youth or childhood. You might be lured to believe that all dogs of this specific breed are precisely the same. You could prevent disappointment by recognizing that each dog is an individual-- much like folks. Your brand-new dog's personality and requirements might be distinct from the dog you had previously, even if he is the identical breed.

You ought to likewise stay away from acquiring a dog entirely since a member of your family desires one. No matter which person is, in fact, in charge of the dog's day-to-day maintenance and upkeep, when a dog lives with a family, he is a part of the household. Just if you understand that he is going to be welcomed by everybody if you buy him and bring him home.

In case you have actually never ever owned a dog previously, your initial dog could be a delight. It does indicate, nevertheless, that you want to do your research well before deciding. You need to understand what to anticipate, and that you are prepared to end up being a dog owner.

Adopting a brand-new dog could be a fantastic experience. Owning a dog could significantly improve your life. When you do a bit of research and use common sense, you are taking the initial step towards obtaining and enjoying a new buddy.

Chapter 1: Breed Comparison

When you consider comparing dog breeds, their size and look might be the primary things you think of. There are numerous other elements involved in picking the dog breed which is appropriate for you.

Comparing breeds includes thinking about your and your family's requirements in addition to your potential pet's. For instance, certain breeds are typically great with kids while others are not. If there are kids in your household, picking a breed of dog which is known for playfulness and gentleness is smarter than picking one which is tougher or aloof. It is a lot more advised to make a sensible decision regarding a breed than to aniticipate your brand-new dog to conform to your household.

As dog breeds have their own personality qualities and traits, you need to select the ideal match for yourself and your household. You might be considering a pet who is going to be a great watchdog, one that is going to be your buddy, or one who likes to play and frolic. When you make a note of your expectations, it is going to be simpler to discover the breed ideally suited to you.

Another crucial point to think about when comparing breeds are health concerns. As numerous purebreds are far more prone to establishing numerous kinds of health issues, understanding which problems pertain to the breed you are thinking about can aid you to stay away from heartache and pricey vet costs. You ought to understand what to anticipate from a certain breed prior to making your decision.

Some breeds need more maintenance than others. Whether it is a matter of regular shedding, or bathing more frequently than others, you could narrow your options down to the breeds, which ideally match your capability to look after a brand-new dog. It is likewise an excellent idea to think about just how much food and other products he is going to require regularly.

When you have considered all these points, there is an extra element which is going to likewise aid you to select the breed that is ideal for you: you wish a dog which you are going to love, and enjoy hanging out with for many years. You might have a specific breed in mind, or you might be waiting to discover the appropriate one. When you remember that you and your brand-new dog are going to develop a mutually-beneficial relationship, you are going to discover the perfect dog breed to welcome into your life.

Chapter 2: Mixed Breed Consideration

Whether you have your heart set on a specific dog breed or are waiting to discover one which appears enticing, there is another option for you to think about. A mixed-breed might be precisely the sort of dog you desire.

Contrary to typical opinion, there is nothing subpar about mixed breed dogs. Not only do they make perfect pets, they are likewise quality animals. In case you have not yet decided on a particular breed, or are considering other possibilities, you may wish to consider adopting a mixed breed dog.

There are certain crucial advantages to mixed breeds. Initially, logically, a mixed breed dog is going to generally be much less costly than its purebred equivalent. If you desire a wonderful pet that does not break your budget, a mixed breed dog might be a great choice for you.

Second, mixed breed dogs do not normally have health issues typically related to lots of purebred dogs. In case you select a mixed breed, it is most likely that he is going to stay healthier far longer.

There are a variety of locations where you could obtain a mixed breed dog. If you have not yet decided what type of dog you desire, you could likewise look around to see what is out there. You could discover ads for mixed dog breeds in almost any newspaper, or you could visit your regional animal shelter. Many individuals promote dogs free-of-charge or at low prices when they are relocating, or for other reasons. Animal shelters have an excess of mixed dog breeds. Lots of animal shelters consist of neutering or spaying, canine immunizations and de-worming for dogs who are adopted.

As individuals have a tendency to prefer purebred dogs, there are great deals of mixed breed dogs who require homes. When you think about adopting a mixed breed dog, you could offer a terrific dog a brand-new home of his own. As a reward, your mixed breed pet is going to be a source of happiness.

Chapter 3: Being Reasonable

An effective adoption suggests is having reasonable expectations, and about what you could provide to your brand-new pet. You are going to have the ideal outcomes if you think about these expectations prior to making the final decision regarding adopting a dog.

Initially, you need to think about what you want from the dog you wish to adopt. The function he is going to play in your life is one factor. Are you trying to find a dog who is going to protect your family and home, one who is going to be your friend, or a dog who is going to get along nicely with other pets and your kids? When you have the responses to these types of questions, it is going to aid you to pick the dog which is ideal for you.

You additionally want to understand the expectations you have concerning your brand-new pet's personality, character, and disposition. You might be trying to find a dog who has a lively personality and is extremely active, or a dog that is calm and peaceful. These elements likewise affect the sort of dog you ought to adopt.

As expectations are a two-way street, you additionally want to consider what you can provide to your brand-new pet. You might have an abundance of spare time to devote to your dog, or a hectic schedule where the quantity of time you are able to dedicate to your dog is going to be rather limited. Even though all dogs require their owners' time, certain dogs are more demanding. This consists of playtime, and time which you need to devote to your dog's maintenance. The dog you pick needs to match your way of life without numerous modifications on either his part or yours.

The lifestyle factor is relevant to your family, too. Which individual is going to be looking after the dog regularly is one example. Whether he is going to be a family dog, or mainly a single person's special pet, the duties for his care must be talked about and agreed upon before you adopt him. In certain families, providing a brand-new pet to a kid is typically viewed as a great way for children to learn about responsibility. Nevertheless, whether your kid is a teenager or a toddler, it is most likely reckless to provide him complete responsibility for his brand-new pet.

Even though establishing a sense of responsibility, and establishing a relationship with a dog could both be great experiences for kids, excessive focus on responsibility might result in him resenting his dog and not caring for him properly. It is essential to be sensible with just how much you can anticipate from the kid.

If your family regularly takes family trips, or if you frequently go away on business trips, these elements have to be thought about. Whether you prepare to take your dog with you on vacation, or need to leave him behind when you take a trip, making decisions ahead of time about how he is going to match your way of life could save confusion, time and even cash, in the future.

The financial commitments of a dog are necessary aspects. Vet expenses, dog food, and other regular parts of dog upkeep must be thought about well before adopting. The maintenance and upkeep of some dogs are more expensive than that of others. You need to understand that you can easily afford him. You would not desire a high-maintenance dog if you are on a minimal budget plan, nor would you desire unanticipated costs after you have actually adopted him.

An effective adoption consists of having proper expectations. You want to understand what you anticipate from him, and what he can fairly anticipate from you. When you place a bit of time into considering these aspects prior to adopting a dog, you are going to be more probable to be entirely pleased with the dog you pick.

If your brand-new pet is going to be living with your whole family, dedicating a bit of time to going over these topics with your household are going to be helpful to everybody concerned. It is going to decrease the possibility of unpredicted surprises, and lead to the adoption being a favorable experience for your brand-new pet and each member of your home. He is going to genuinely be a nice addition to your household.

Chapter 4: Networking

You might not have actually considered networking as being a fundamental part of dog adoption. There are a variety of reasons why networking could lead to more success with adoption. It coučd assist you in picking the best dog, and improve the the dog owner experience.

Before you, in fact, adopt a dog, you could find out a great deal about the breed by networking with individuals who currently have one. While there are numerous excellent ways to learn more about dogs, absolutely nothing is better than first-hand experience. You could network with owners, either face to face or online, and get really favorable outcomes. The majority of dog owners are going to like to share information with you, along with private stories about life with their pet. You could get a wealth of important input and information from dog owners, and you might even make some new buddies.

Networking is likewise excellent after you have actually adopted your new dog and taken him home. In numerous circumstances, the most effective way to get guidance and the responses to questions is from individuals who have actually owned a dog for a long period of time. They could be the perfect information source, in addition to friendships based upon your shared interest.

Regardless of what sort of dog you are thinking about, it is likely that you could discover online clubs and forums dedicated to your specific dog breed and their owners. In some areas, you might even have the ability to discover clubs not far from where you reside.

Along with these casual methods of networking, you might likewise have an interest in the American Kennel Club or a comparable organization. The American Kennel Club is the ideal source for whatever you want to understand about your dog breed. They likewise offer listings of clubs for particular breeds, breeder listings, and a lot more. No matter the breed, you have actually picked, the American Kennel Club is your finest source of both information and chances for networking.

Chapter 5: Doing the Research

The more you understand about the dog you adopt, the more pleased you are going to be about your choice. Acquiring the facts by researching the breed you have actually picked is a necessary step in being pleased with your brand-new pet. There are certain key points that you ought to search for as you are looking into a breed.

If you have actually chosen to adopt a purebred, you might have little or much interest in the pedigree. Nevertheless, even if you do not consider it to be an essential element, you must still get all of the information. You can ask for a copy of the dog's pedigree documents, which ought to consist of all of the information about his bloodline and parentage. As numerous purebred dog breeders own the parents of the pups they have for sale, going to your new dog's parents could be a favorable experience.

It is a great idea to be cautious of breeders or particular dog owners who specify that their dog is a purebred yet do not have documents as evidence of this. While they might be entirely truthful, the likelihood that they are not is a thing to remember prior to consenting to adopting the dog.

When you are looking into the breed you have actually selected, the main points are to assist you in choosing if this is the appropriate breed, and what to expect from possessing your new pet. You could research on the web, by speaking with owners and breeders, and by going to the dog section in your library.

Finding out about your breed's history could be an informing experience. Whether you have an interest in elements as where the breed came from or not, there is important information to be discovered in the breed's history. One instance is the breed that has actually been reproduced for a particular purpose. Not just are you going to discover this fascinating, it is going to additionally aid you to comprehend your dog's character, mindset, and personality.

What could you discover in the history of a breed? The truths you come up with might be astonishing! The dog you adopt might be the descendant of dogs owned by royalty, dogs that were mainly utilized as work animals, or dogs that were picked as guardians. The more you understand about where your breed originated from, the more you are going to comprehend how the pet you pick matches your life today.

Looking into a breed consists of finding out about the requirements for this specific breed. Even if you are thinking no further than acquiring an excellent buddy, you might desire the greatest instance of your breed. A bit of research is going to supply information on the elements which constitute top requirements in markings and color, body tone, size, and other physical attributes. The highest quality dog is going to fulfill these requirements.

As you have actually already read, purebred dogs are able to feature a range of health problems. Prior to adopting a purebred, exploring the health concerns typically related to your breed can assist you to choose if you wish to take this risk, and to be ready beforehand. You want to understand whether your breed is susceptible to establishing health conditions from bone issues to cancer, and how you are going to handle such conditions if they do take place.

If these issues do not prevent you from adopting the breed of your choice, you might want to look into buying medical insurance for your pet when you adopt him. You are going to then be much better prepared for both the financial and the psychological elements of health issues, and your dog is going to have a much better possibility for a longer life expectancy.

You wish for the experience of owning a dog to be favorable for both yourself and your brand-new pet. When you do a small bit of research beforehand, the experience could be a great one undoubtedly! You could acquire a much better understanding of your dog before he ends up being a part of your family. When you have all of this essential understanding beforehand, you can concentrate on taking pleasure in numerous years together with your brand-new pet.

Chapter 6: Getting to Know Your Dog

Regardless of just how much time you place into finding out about the breed you have selected, there is an extra point which you must think about: while there are numerous elements common to a specific breed, every dog is still an individual. You could acquire a reasonable amount of understanding of what the breed is like, however, learning more about your own dog indicates going a bit further.

The most effective method to learn more about your dog is with in-person visits prior to making your last decision to adopt. If the breeder you have actually selected lives relatively close to you, or if you have the ability to travel, the time you place into this is going to be indispensable. When you are able to meet, visit, and hang out with a dog, you are going to have the ability to identify if he is the appropriate "fit" for you.

Spending simply a small amount of time in your dog's company is going to assist you in seeing what his character and habits are like. You might discover that you and he are a great match right away, that you grow to love one another, or that there are clashes which push you to choose that this is not the appropriate dog for you. If you have the chance to do so, meeting and hanging out with the dog prior to adopting is going to be really beneficial.

You might be thinking about a breeder who lives too far to go to personally. In this circumstance, hanging out with your dog prior to adopting him might not be possible. You are going to need to rely on the breeder to provide the information you require. Even though dog breeders are busy, an excellent breeder is going to be more than happy to interact with you, and respond to all of your concerns. His objective is not just to discover a great home for his dog, but to have a pleased client too.

Asking questions about the dog's routines and way of life assists you to see whether he is an excellent match for you. One instance is to ask whether the dog has actually been raised in his breeder's house, outdoors, or in a kennel. This is going to let you understand what type of daily environment the dog is familiar with, and whether the environment you prepare for him is comparable or different.

Another question for the breeder is how the dog engages with individuals and other pets. A dog who has actually been looked after in his breeder's house might be accustomed to being around kids, grownups, and other animals, while the dog who has actually been outdoors or in a kennel might not. The function of understanding these points beforehand is to assist you in choosing whether the dog you are considering can quickly get used to your house circumstance, or whether it might produce excessive problems.

The breeder ought to likewise want to talk about the dog's routines with you. You might be intending to adopt a pup, or a grown-up dog. Each of these age groups, or phases, comes with assets and unique concerns. For instance, while a puppy could be expected to have "mishaps" on the floor, the adult-aged dog ought to be totally trained. An adult-aged dog is already affected by years of experiences, which could impact his mindset and habits, while a little puppy is waiting for experiences to form his mindsets, habits, and character.

You wish to know what your dog is truly like prior to bringing him home. If there are unfavorable elements to your dog's habits and routines, learning about them beforehand assists you in preparing to manage them. You might choose that this is the dog you have actually been searching for, or you might alter your mind and carry on with your search somewhere else. In either case, the ideal time to find out about your dog is prior to, in fact, adopting him.

If you have the ability to choose, it is much better to select a dog and breeder whom you can meet before adopting. While it is feasible to get a good deal of information over the phone, via letters, or by communicating online with the breeder, it is no match for hanging out with your potential brand-new pet personally. This is going to provide you the chance to see him in the environment he is familiar with, see how he engages with individuals, and observe him at play.

Whichever technique is suitable for your circumstance, the most vital point to bear in mind is to discover as much as you are able to about the dog you wish to adopt prior to agreeing to buy him. It can assist you to avoid making the error of acquiring a dog that is all inappropriate for you, and make the chances very good that you are going to discover the dog who is the ideal fit for you.

Chapter 7: Getting Ready for the New Dog!

In the most ideal of scenarios, each member of your household is as delighted about the possibility of a brand-new pet joining the family as you are. Nevertheless, so as to make this terrific occasion as thrilling as it could be, it does call for some prep work.

Preparing your home for your pet's grand entryway could be an experience in itself. You wish to make certain that your home is safe and comfy for your brand-new dog, in addition to lowering the threat of damage to your home from your brand-new canine member of the family. Neither of these elements of pet ownership are hard, yet they do take a bit of time, initiative, and perceptiveness.

A great way to start preparing your home resembles preparing it for a kid. Starting on the floor, and working upward, look for anything which might possibly hurt your pet, or which he might ruin. If you have many device cables or electrical wires which he might chew, they ought to be relocated to where he can't get to them or made hard to reach. If you have items which could be easilysmashed or broken, these too must be relocated to where your dog can not get to them. These safety measures have to apply to each room in your house where your dog is going to be spending the time.

Kids have to be warned not to leave their toys and other personal things where the dog is able to obtain them. This is to make sure that their property is not going to be damaged, along with your brand-new pet not being hurt by chewing up or swallowing things. Puppies and grown-up dogs alike could choke on foreign items, and many have the propensity to chew on anything that is out there.

When you are prepping your home for the dog you are adopting, it is an excellent idea to concentrate on a special location only for him. A brand-new pet is going to feel comfortable much faster if he understands where everything of his own lies. His water and food meals, toys, and paper, if he is to be paper trained, are ideally put in one particular area and left there. He is going to quickly find out that these things belong to him, and where he can constantly locate them. This fundamental sense of regimen is going to provide your brand-new dog convenience and stability, even throughout his initial days in your home.

Preparing your household for the dog you are adopting could likewise be thrilling. When each member of your household is included, your brand-new dog is going to be well-received as a fresh member of the household.

It is an excellent idea to give kids lots of preparation for the dog. While information about what to expect, what the dog is going to be like, and other bits of interest are going to boost your kids' anticipation, they likewise have to be filled in on the correct care and treatment of the dog prior to moving into your home. Kids, particularly, need to be instructed on such elements as not being extremely lively around the brand-new dog, to not yank his tail, and to be kind with him. This is for the security of the kids along with the dog.

If your kids are sufficiently old, providing them a tiny amount of responsibility for the dog's daily care could likewise be helpful. They are going to understand they are contributing something beneficial to their pet's maintenance. Something as fundamental as filling the dog's food bowl, even with your guidance, increases kids' satisfaction of owning a pet.

Identifying ahead of time, and discussing with the entire family, who is going to be accountable for most of the dog's day-to-day care and upkeep could prevent lapse of memory and arguments in the future. Maybe each family member can be appointed a task, or maybe you pick to handle the majority of it yourself. Whichever arrangement is ideal for your household, deciding beforehand is better.

When should you start prepping your family and home for the brand-new dog? The quicker, the better is an excellent way to look at it! By doing this, you are not going to run the risk of being caught off guard by forgetting something crucial about preparing your home, nor the issues which might take place from having a new pet move in before your household is prepared for him.

On the other hand, the better prepared you are for the new arrival, the more thrilling the whole experience is going to be for everybody in your household. They are going to be ready to welcome him, assist him to feel comfortable, and take pleasure in each minute of dog ownership.

Chapter 8: Buying the Supplies

There is a lot more to owning a dog than toys and food. Considering the supplies he is going to require well ahead of bringing him home, guarantees you a smooth shift from living without a dog to having one feel entirely at home with you. While the dog breed you are adopting is relevant to the supplies he is going to require, you could begin with the essentials and change them to whatever is suitable for your breed.

Food and water meals are available in 3 standard styles. These consist of individual meals, connected meals, and meals which hold and dispense the items. You can choose which design is more practical for you.

Dogs typically fare better if they are regularly provided with one type of dog food. Along with dry, canned, and dog food that requires including water, there are a lot of various kinds on the market. From natural dog food with no artificial components, to dog food with additional vitamins, to dog food specifically produced for a dog's age, you could feel rather overwhelmed when attempting to select the appropriate one for your brand-new pet. Even if you have actually owned dogs previously, it is an excellent idea to ask your vet to suggest the most suitable dog food for your new dog.

Grooming supplies likewise belong on your list of products to buy prior to bringing your pet home. While the particular supplies you buy depend upon the sort of dog you are adopting, a lot of dogs do need some amount of upkeep. A brush which is just for him, non-toxic shampoo created specifically for puppies or dogs, and his personal bath towel, are the essentials.

Your dog might gain from health aids, like vitamin supplements. They could assist even the healthiest pet to remain at his finest. You could ask your vet or the breeder about the particular kind of supplements he ought to have. They might advise you to feed him vitamin-fortified dog food, or different supplements.

Naturally, your new pet requires toys. Not just will toys provide him the opportunity to have fun and play, it could additionally reduce his desire to chew on your personal belongings and furnishings. If you get him some toys that he can have fun with by himself, in addition to toys to utilize throughout his playtime with you, he is going to be more pleased and not so harmful.

When you are picking toys for your brand-new dog, there are 2 points to bear in mind. Initially, pick toys which are suitable for your dog's breed, size, and age. For instance, a toy which is fit for a big dog is worthless to a puppy. Second, while toys that are created particularly for dogs are non-toxic and solid, examining them prior to purchasing them can prevent catastrophe. Staying away from toys created from wood which can splinter, anything that might break or shatter, and toys with little parts or paint, is definitely vital.

Dog treats are an outstanding inclusion to your supply list. Whether you intend to train your new dog for a particular function, or only desire him to have a little something extra, your dog is going to enjoy his treats. You could discover healthy dog treats created with your pet's age and size in mind.

Lots of dog owners find rawhide items helpful. One benefit of rawhide is that it benefits your dog's teeth. Another advantage is that rawhide is going to accommodate your dog's natural propensity to chew, so he is not going to be utilizing your shoes or other personal belongings for this function. Rawhide items are available in several sizes and designs. Picking the rawhide items matched to your dog's breed and size is the ideal method to guarantee that he receives all of the benefits from these chewing items.

When you are prepping your supply list, you want to choose whether your dog is going to utilize a dog bed, or whether you prefer other plans. Some dogs take to dog beds right away, while others do not like them whatsoever. If you want him to utilize a dog bed, it is necessary to pick the appropriate size and product. This is going to make him more comfy, as well as lead to your dog being more probable to utilize it. Nevertheless, while his convenience is important, the bed you pick ought to likewise be simple to tidy and practically unbreakable. The better the condition his bed is in, the more pleased he is going to be to sleep in it. It is likewise much healthier for him.

As it is risky to permit any dog to wander openly outdoors, you ought to plan on taking your dog for walks regularly. This assures him of obtaining adequate exercise, along with establishing a favorable relationship with you. The collar and leash, need to be suitable to his age and size. He has to be restrained throughout his walks, without pain. As these items are offered in a range of weights, sizes, and components, make certain to have your pet's age and size in mind when you buy them.

Buying supplies for your brand-new pet is easy, and does not have to be pricey. When you draw up your list beforehand, you could do some comparison shopping for great values. Having all of the supplies in your home before your dog gets there is the most effective method to guarantee his pleasure, health, and joy right from the beginning.

Chapter 9: Where to Find Breeders?

There are numerous reasons why it is essential to do a bit of comparisons and research before picking a breeder. You must never ever agree to do business with the initial breeder you discover. Adopting the dog which is appropriate for you implies putting a bit of effort and time into discovering the appropriate breeder.

Initially, certain breeders are just not as good as others. You are going to even discover those who breed dogs for a living who are not up to par. They do not take appropriate dog care, and could be less than truthful about health issues or other problems. You desire a breeder who takes outstanding dog care, attends to their requirements, and really likes the dogs he owns and offers. This is another advantage to meeting and going to your breeder ahead of time. When a breeder likes and looks after his dogs, it is apparent instantly.

Second, working with the initial breeder you discover could be an error economically. If you do not do some window shopping initially, you might be uninformed of just how much the dogs typically cost. At its worst, a dishonest breeder could make the most of this, and attempt to charge you far more for the dog. You might wind up paying substantially more for your brand-new pet than you ought to.

There are 2 preferred techniques for discovering breeders. One is by getting suggestions from other dog owners who were pleased with their experiences and have actually adopted quality pets. This is one topic where networking is going to help you. If you do not know anybody personally who has actually bought a dog from a breeder, you could get input and great recommendations from owners on internet forums and dog clubs.

The other approach of discovering a breeder is via the American Kennel Club. The American Kennel Club has a continuous, updated breeder list for practically any dog breed you have an interest in adopting.

After you have actually discovered breeders, doing some window shopping is going to aid you in discovering the ideal dog and the ideal value. Even if somebody has actually been personally suggested to you, or appears on the American Kennel Club's listings, comparing a variety of breeders is going to offer you the outcomes you desire.

Comparing breeders indicates preparing your questions and getting considerate, direct, truthful responses. While the expense of the dog are a top priority, it is far from being the only subject to deal with. There are other elements which go into an effective adoption. An excellent breeder is not going to think twice in responding to any and all of your questions.

The breeder ought to be willing to fill you in entirely about his work. This consists of such elements as how long he has actually been breeding this specific type of dog, both the favorable and unfavorable experiences he has actually had, and whether it is his full-time job or a pastime. If he has actually been breeding dogs for an extended time period, and shows that it has actually been an excellent experience, you are more probable to get a dog that has actually been properly looked after by this individual.

The breeder ought to likewise be really educated about the breed, and happy to share this information. From special personality peculiarities related to the dogs and prospective health issues, he is going to want you to understand everything about the type of dog you are adopting. Not only is this useful to you, it additionally reveals that has the experience with the breed.

If you have actually selected a breed which is usually utilized for a particular function, you might be adopting a dog with this function in mind or you might not. For instance, you might have your heart set on a gorgeous hunting dog just since you like this sort of dog, but with no intent of utilizing him for hunting. You might desire a breed that is mostly utilized as a show dog, but desire him for a household pet instead.

The breeder who handles these types of dogs ought to take your desires into consideration. Several breeders are not going to sell their dogs to potential owners who want them for a separate reason. It is necessary to be straight up with the breeder concerning the function you want to have for your brand-new dog. If your plan for your dog is suitable, it should not stand in the way of adoption. However, if a breeder is firm about just selling his dogs for a particular function, you may wish to think about searching for another breeder.

An excellent breeder is likewise happy to interact with you after the adoption. This reveals that his interest does not stop with the sale. He would like to know that both his client and the dog are joyful, comfy with the brand-new plan, and entirely pleased with the adoption. When these elements are clear in your preliminary interactions with the breeder, it is a great indication that you have actually discovered the appropriate one.

For all of these reasons, you must never ever opt for the initial breeder you discover. You are going to have an effective adoption when you do some comparisons initially. The breeder is going to be pleased to understand his dog has an excellent home, and you and your brand-new pet are going to both be ready for a new life together.

Chapter 10: Is Your Dog Well?

An effective adoption implies adopting a dog which is in exceptional condition. It is vital for his comfort, health, and relationship with his brand-new owner.

Asking the breeder for a health certificate is a great start. You likewise want to understand what the health certificate covers. At its finest, the dog should have been inspected by a vet to guarantee his general good health. He ought to be devoid of any health problems and health conditions. The dog you adopt has to have a variety of immunizations suitable for his age. The de-worming treatments ideal for his age should be performed prior to adopting him. All of these elements enter into adopting a dog which is in perfect condition.

An excellent breeder is going to likewise supply a written warranty of the dog's condition and health when you choose to adopt. Depending upon the specific breeder, this could consist of an agreement to refund your cash or exchange the dog for a separate one. These guarantees are generally legitimate for a particular length of time.

Even if the breeder has actually provided you a health certificate, it is still an excellent idea to have your brand-new dog inspected by your own vet. There are 2 essential reasons for this. Initially, it is going to supply you with the assurance of understanding that your brand-new pet is entirely healthy. Second, it is going to assist you in establishing a relationship with the vet.

Selecting an excellent vet needs to be on your list of things to do when preparing to adopt a dog. If you do not currently have one, you want to discover the one who is finest matched to you and your brand-new pet. An excellent vet is not going to object to you touring his establishments, and is going to be pleased to address your concerns.

As you and your vet are going to be in one another's lives for your pet's sake, a great rapport is not just beneficial, but vital. As you most likely select a family doctor by choosing the one you were comfy with, the same holds true when picking a vet for your dog. Engaging with you in a respectful, expert manner is a favorable indication. Comprehending that you have numerous questions, and want to put in the time to address them, is another.

If you have the chance to observe the vet and his personnel with other animals, it could be extremely useful. You can see how they deal with the animals, and how they engage with them. The vet and his personnel who regularly reveal generosity and real concern for their patients are the ones you are able to trust with your dog. The vet or personnel who show impatience ought to be steered clear of.

The vet you pick ought to either be available for emergency situations, or offer you with the information on another vet to call. While a couple of them are on-call all the time, you want to understand what to do if an emergency situation takes place after-hours, holidays or during weekends.

Your vet ought to supply you with all of the information you require for your dog's continuous health. This consists of letting you understand when your pet has to have his immunizations updated, the ideal method to handle any health issues, and how to prevent unneeded health issues. The vet who displays a genuine interest in your dog is the ideal option.

While your dog's physical condition and health make for effective adoption, his mental condition is just as important. Even though a great breeder keeps his dogs mentally fit, your brand-new dog might come with mindsets or behavioral issues which you had not taken into consideration when you adopted him. This is another reason why checking out your dog prior to adopting him is a great idea, if it is feasible. If not, you might want to count on the breeder for total sincerity about these problems.

Even a dog who has actually been treated properly and looked after appropriately by his breeder could be challenging. He might be aggressive, moody, aloof, or perhaps depressed. Adopting him and bringing him into a new setting could boost these sorts of issues. When you learn about them ahead of time, it can aid you to take his special requirements into consideration. You may choose to adopt a different dog completely, or make adjustments for your brand-new dog to fit better into your home and be more comfy.

The physical and mental condition of your brand-new dog can suggest the difference between an effective adoption and distress. You desire the ideal dog you can get, and to be certain that all sensible safety measures have actually been taken for him to have a healthy, long, delighted life. The tiny amount of time that you invest in making sure he is in fine condition is going to benefit both you and your dog for years to come. Life with your new buddy is going to be the terrific experience you are eagerly anticipating.

Chapter 11: Your Dog is an Investment!

When you looked into the dog breed you have actually picked, you might have been shocked to discover it to have a long life expectancy. This is one reason why adopting a dog must never ever be performed on an impulse or without mindful preparation. Your dog is a long-lasting investment-- with appropriate care, he is going to be a part of your life long into the future. The more you prepare for this, the more pleasant the experience is going to be for you and your new dog.

The word "investment" might evoke financial issues. While this is far from being the only element, it is definitely one to consider. Understanding that you are prepared for long-lasting financial investment is a standard part of dog adoption. You need to consider his everyday maintenance, his regular health care, and whether you are ready for any injuries or diseases which might take place all of a sudden.

Although dog food and regular vet visits can accumulate, getting ready for the unforeseen by buying medical insurance for your dog is an excellent investment. You are not going to have to fret about an unexpected health problem or mishap causing vet expenses that you can not pay for, or risk overlooking his health due to the fact that health care is too costly.

The long-term investment of a brand-new dog likewise entails your time. A lot of individuals adopt dogs, just to be dissatisfied when they understand that they do not have ample time for their brand-new pets. The busiest schedules could accommodate a dog, if you plan for his requirements ahead of time.

One instance is the dog who needs a considerable quantity of attention and time. This might be a puppy, and a senior dog, or a breed which is naturally more requiring than others. You have to understand beforehand that you can dedicate sufficient time to your pet prior to bringing him home. You likewise want to decide that providing your time and your focus to the dog is going to be a favorable experience and enjoyment. Nobody ought to feel strained by their pets, as this makes dog ownership unfavorable and demanding for both the dog and the owner.

If your busy schedule consists of travel or long work hours, it is essential to think about how to handle this prior to adopting. The dog who does not get enough of his owner's focus and time is not obtaining what he is worthy of. He can end up being hard, and his health might suffer. The busy person who wishes to adopt should think about the quantity of time he can routinely provide to his brand-new pet, and choose if he has to ask another member of the family or buddy for help with the dog when he can not be there personally. A dog can feel disregarded even if all of his material requirements are provided, when he does not get ample attention and time.

Adopting a brand-new dog is likewise an investment of yourself. When it concerns investing your friendship, love and companionship, what you can provide is going to show in its outcomes. The most effective method to guarantee an effective adoption is for you and your whole family to be pleased with the possibility of including a new member to your home, and being consistent with these sensations for as long as your dog resides with you.

The dog which is appreciated and valued is the dog that is content and happiest. When you show delight and good spirits engaging with your pet, it is never ever going to go undetected. The relationship you extend to him daily is going to be well-received, and offered to you in return. Despite a dog's breed or age, the dog who is appreciated by his owner is completely mindful of it.

The bottom line in making the long-lasting investment of dog adoption is that you have to think further than today. If you have any uncertainties about your capability to attend to and look after him for several years to come, now is the time to reflect on your choice to adopt. Equally crucial, if you have any doubts about whether your willingness to have a dog might alter in the coming years, please do not be too rash to adopt one. Not just is quitting on a dog who has actually lived with his owner awhile a tragic experience for the owner, it is painful to the dog too. It does not take long for a brand-new pet to come to like his owner-- so make certain you are not going to change your mind.

After you have actually taken the elements of this long-lasting investment into consideration, you have a fundamental idea of what owning a dog is going to involve. When you have actually decided to invest yourself and years of your life in a new pet, you are prepared to start the remarkable experience of dog ownership. It is not going to be long before you start to get all of the benefits of sharing your life with a canine buddy.

Concluding Chapter: Bringing Him Home

You now understand all you have to understand to be successful at dog adoption. You have actually discovered the dog you desire, and are restless to bring him home. This is undoubtedly among the most thrilling days in your life! Nevertheless, every grand occasion is not without some level of apprehension. You might be questioning if you are prepared for this obligation. You might be worrying that your household is not ready. You do not want these types of concerns and issues to ruin your dog's homecoming, or get in the way of your initial hours and days together. Besides, you have actually been anticipating this day since you initially began considering adopting a brand-new dog.

The bright side is that you can leave your concerns behind. You are ready and all set for the new member of your family. All you have to do is make a couple of spot-checks, and you are going to be happy about your choice to adopt.

If you are the dog's exclusive owner, preparing a bit of special time only for him is going to help you both. It is an excellent idea to bring your dog home on a weekend or throughout a vacation, when work and other responsibilities are not going to distract from time with your brand-new pet. The more personalized time you are able to commit to him throughout his initial days in your home, the better it is going to be for him. When it is obvious to your brand-new dog that you are glad you picked him, it is going to help you both from the beginning.

A calm, peaceful environment is ideal for welcoming a brand-new dog, and assisting him in feeling safe and comfy. Loud or constant sounds, a flurry of activity, and other interruptions ought to be avoided as much as feasible. He is going to understand that he is moving into a serene, great environment.

Whether your brand-new dog is going to have access to your whole house or not, taking him to his own personal space immediately is an excellent start. He has to end up being acquainted with, and familiarized with, his water and food meals, his toys, and his bed. When he instantly discovers where his special belongings lie, this is the primary step in making him feel comfortable.

If there are other members of your family, familiarizing them with your brand-new dog could be an exciting experience for everybody concerned. It is usually ideal to present your pet to individuals one by one. This is going to aid him to not feel overloaded, in addition to providing him the opportunity to get to know each specific person. He is going to quickly start to accept everybody as his brand-new family.

Kids in your household need to be advised on how to make your dog's very initial days in your home worry-free, comfy, and enjoyable. It might not be an excellent idea to leave kids alone with the dog up until they are familiar with one another. Rather, you can monitor and note how they engage.

Kids of all ages have to be advised not to be rowdy or make loud noises around the brand-new dog. Even if the dog is to end up being their buddy, they need to be mild, mindful, and peaceful throughout his initial days in your home. This is going to aid in preventing him from being scared of the kids, and set the groundwork for a great relationship between the kids and your dog.

A fast spot-check to make certain you have all of his supplies on hand and prepared for him is going to guarantee that you did not forget something. Similar to being prepared for a brand-new human family member, when you understand you are totally ready for his arrival, it could be the magnificent occasion you have actually been waiting for. You, and each member of your household, can go from anticipation to having a pleased, comfy brand-new addition to your family.

Whether you have actually put a number of weeks or numerous months into whatever it requires for successful adoption, the day you bring him home is going to just strengthen your decision. When he gets in your home, and understands that it is now his home, you have a companion and buddy to treasure for the remainder of his life.

I hope that you enjoyed reading through this book and that you have found it useful. If you want to share your thoughts on this book, you can do so by leaving a review on the Amazon page. Have a great rest of the day.

Printed in Great Britain
by Amazon